AF422122

FLY

AN ANTHOLOGY OF POETRY

FLY

AN ANTHOLOGY OF POETRY

CONTENTS

CONTEST WINNERS

FLY

AN ANTHOLOGY OF POETRY

MARCIE FLINCHUM ATKINS

ABOUT THE CONTRIBUTOR

Marcie Flinchum Atkins is a teacher-librarian by day and a children's book writer in the wee hours of the morning. She holds an M.A. and M.F.A. in Children's Literature from Hollins University. She is the author of several nonfiction books, including Wait, Rest, Pause: Dormancy in Nature (Millbrook Press, 2019). Marcie's poetry for children has also been featured in several anthologies. For more information about Marcie's books and poetry, visit her at www.marcieatkins.com and on Twitter and Instagram @marciefatkins.

UNTITLED

purple milkweed buds

tightly bound—a week away

from monarchs

BENJAMIN BISHOP

ABOUT THE CONTRIBUTOR

Benjamin Bishop is a married father of three children and resides in Southern California, where he enjoys the beach and camping.

Benjamin teaches English Language Arts and has both a Bachelor's and Master's in English Literature.

Benjamin was co-winner of the 2023 Haiku Contest on TheHumanist.com, has fiction and poetry published in *Clever Fox Literary Magazine*, and is currently working on his own upcoming poetry collection, *A Ballad of Yesterday and Tomorrow*.

BLINK

Like the butterfly

Transforming before your eyes

Life is but a blink.

Patricia Cooley

ABOUT THE CONTRIBUTOR

Patricia Cooley is an author, educator, and storyteller. She has taught reading and writing to K-8 students for over 30 years. She holds a Professional Educational License with endorsements in elementary education, secondary education, administration, gifted education, Spanish, English, and Language Arts.

She has studied poetry and writing at the Institute of Children's Literature, Society for Children's Book Writers and Illustrators, Lyrical Language Lab, 12 X 12 Book Challenge, Highlights Foundation, Children's Book Insider, Pomelo classes, the ABCs of Poetry, and ongoing conferences.

Patricia's publications include:

And the Crowd Goes Wild; A Global Anthology of Sports Poems

Highlights Hello, High Five, and High Five Bilingue Magazines

Teacher in Focus

Stories for Children

MONARCH MANIFEST

Monarch

Symbolizes

Hope

Upcoming

Transformation

Newness

Direction

Change

Life

Unlived

Yet.

LINDA M. CRATE

ABOUT THE CONTRIBUTOR

Linda M. Crate (she/her) is a Pennsylvanian writer whose poetry, short stories, articles, and reviews have been published in a myriad of magazines both online and in print. She has twelve published chapbooks, the latest being: *Searching Stained Glass Windows For An Answer* (Alien Buddha Publishing, December 2022). She is also the author of the novella *Mates* (Alien Buddha Publishing, March 2022). Her debut book of photography, *Songs of the Creek* (Alien Buddha Publishing, April 2023), was recently published.

INTROVERTED AND CAUTIOUS

once there were severalmonarch butterflies
dancing across my parents' lawn,

and i couldn't help but watch
them dancing on the purple and pink
clovers in the field;

few were prey to my camera
as i tried to take photos
of these beautiful
creatures—

tiger swallowtails, in my experience,
are friendlier;

they have followed me on walks
and allowed me to photograph them and
seem curious of me—

monarchs are more introverted
and cautious.

UNDERSTANDING

once there was
a spicebush
swallowtail
flying around one of
my parents' bushes,

about to fly away;
i asked him or her to wait
and much to my surprise
they did—

only stopping to allow me one
photograph before they
flew away to some place my
eyes could not be quick enough
to follow,

and i thought how wonderful a
butterfly would listen to a request
from another being;

i wonder if they understand more
than we give them credit for.

SWALLOWTAIL DANCE

i remember once
looking at a wild
rose thinking of how
lovely she was,

and then a tiger swallowtail
danced across my hand
and onto the rose;

he or she allowed me to photograph her
before fluttering by on their way

flying away with their vibrant
yellow wings into some
amber song of the sun—

and i couldn't help but smile
because i couldn't help but think
of how lovely the butterfly was
to include me.

ENCOUNTER WITH A
MOURNING CLOAK

monarch butterflies
are no stranger
to my grandmother's flower
garden,

but once a mourning cloak
decided to visit instead;

and i got a few pictures
of it when it landed on
the grill beneath one of my gran's
hanging flower baskets

she is fond of having in the summer—

it was the first time i saw a
mourning cloak,
but maybe they were others that
hung around me i didn't see because
they blend into the environment better than the
orange-winged monarch.

I LIKE MEMENTOS

monarch butterflies
like milkweed,
but they also like
clovers;

i saw them dancing in the
gravel once of my parents' yard
before they decided to snack
on the yard clover—

i wonder what they were
discussing as they danced together
in that large circle of wings,

but it was a beautiful feast for the eyes;
a song that my heart cannot forget—

i always try to capture moments in
photographs,
but my mother says that sometimes
you have to be present to appreciate the moment;

not everything can be photographed—

and i know she's right,
but sometimes i like mementos
of memories so i can look back
and smile.

ROBERT DANIEL

ABOUT THE CONTRIBUTOR

Robert Daniel lives in Alabama and spends most of his time working as an engineer and providing for his wife and kids. When he's not working, he's busy on the homestead, rarely on social media, and trying to keep his kids off the phone too. He has only just started pursuing a life-long passion for writing. *Fly* and *Wild* are his first poetry publications.

Robert Daniel

BUTTERFLIES OVER BEES

For halloween, my sister
dressed up as a bee. I don't
like bees. They sting and
buzz too close and get caught
in my hair. She was annoying
like a bee, always humming
in my ears. There was another girl,
but she was a butterfly.
Every time we trick-or-treated
at the same house, all the adults
said they liked her costume.
I think that hurt my sister's feelings.
When it kept happening, she
finally screamed that she had more
candy than the girl. In response,
the girl dumped all the sweets from
my sister's bucket onto the ground.
Even after that, I think we still preferred
to have more butterflies in the world.

VEINS

In high school,
I had a teacher who
wore a thick band on her wrist.
Rumors about it floated through the class.
Was it a scar from a cut she had made?
Was our science teacher so depressed
that she'd commit suicide
and not return one day?
I had seen it once
while we prepped for an experiment.
She had taken off the band
to wash her hands.
Small, black lines that looked like veins
carved into her skin—wings.
The most beautiful tattoo I'd ever seen,
and she had to cover it up.

Robert Daniel

THE COLLAGE

A collection on his wall.
Is it art? Or is it science?
The *Hesperiidae*, looks
like a moth, but holds its
wings like a butterfly.
Could it be both?
Five more that need to be
examined and pinned.
They were already dead.
Delicately, he stuck one
tail-like wing of the
Papilionidae and then the other
on to the board. Preserved.
In his journal, details,
illustrations with data
that would help understand
them. He placed glass over
their stiff bodies and
filled the wall's empty
spaces with their colors.
Blue so blue was the *Lycaenidae*
that he relocated the frame,
but no matter where, his eyes
were always drawn
to its bright pigmentation.
He knew them all so well.
One always evaded him
as it should, for it was
the king, *Danaus Plexippus.*

SYMMETRY

My face,
two eyes, two ears,
a nose, a mouth.
The same on both sides,
except for the scar
that runs from my brow
to the corner of my lip.
Everyone stared—
makeup couldn't cover it.
Perfectly unsymmetrical.
I swear I saw a butterfly
that had the same blemish
carefully etched across
its wing from tip to body.
Struggling, it fluttered
across the yard and
disappeared over the fence.
Perfectly unsymmetrically
stunning.

LESLIE DEGNAN

ABOUT THE CONTRIBUTOR

Leslie Degnan is a former teacher who writes picture books and poems for children. Her poems have been published in anthologies such as *What is Family?* (2023) and *Hop To It: Poems to Get You Moving* (2020). When she's not writing, you'll find her outdoors birdwatching from her kayak or listening to birdsong in the meadow. You can find her on Twitter @DegnanLeslie.

Leslie Degnan

CATERPILLAR (WC:65)

Caterpillar green and lumpy,
Creep along your milkweed floor.

Your small house is growing frumpy,
As you munch its leafy door.

All the leaves are disappearing.
You are hungry, you can't stop.

I should not be interfering,
But suggest a fresh leaf swap.

In the name of conservation,
All I ask is that you try.

You may have a transformation,
And become a butterfly!

LINDA A. DRYFHOUT

ABOUT THE CONTRIBUTOR

Linda A. Dryfhout is a poet and children's author. Her poetry has been published in Hello, High Five and Highlights magazines. Anthologies include *What Is A Friend?*; *Things We Eat, Things We Do, Hop To It: Poems To Get You Moving*; *Poetry Friday Anthology for Celebrations*, and *Two Truths and A Fib*. Twitter @LADryfhout

HEADING SOUTH

Migration begins
in the early fall.
We huddle up tight.
On a tree, we sprawl.

We try to stay warm,
but on the next day.
Our journey awaits.
We flutter away.

MONARCH BUTTERFLY

Orange, black and white,
etched on silk gossamer wings.
Butterfly flutters.

MONARCH EMERSION

On a milkweed patch
caterpillars hatch.

Chrysalises begin
in a cocoon skin.

After time has passed,
they emerge at last.

They hang there and cling,
pumping fluid to each wing.

Soon it's time to take flight.
They flutter from sight.

JOAN DURIS

ABOUT THE CONTRIBUTOR

Joannie Duris enjoys exploring our world and the world of imagination, never knowing what everyday wonders she might discover right outside her door. She is a children's book author and retired psych nurse. Credits include her first picture book, *B is for Berkshires* (Islandport Press, 2015), and poems in two anthologies from Writers' Loft Press: *Friends & Anemones* (2020) and *Gnomes & UnGnomes* (Nov. 2023).

Joannie keeps busy as a Nordic ski patroller, avid gardener, hiker, bowler, and, of course, writer. She lives in central MA with her husband and spoiled cats, where she occasionally chases black bears away from her birdfeeders. Find out more at www.joanduris.com.

MONARCH CATERPILLAR

Chomp
      Chomp
            Chomp
      Chomp
Chomp

One large
milkweed leaf,
gone in five minutes…
poison for others,
but not for me.
YUM!

NATURE'S MIXED-UP MIRACLE

Nature had some strange
ideas when she created me…
She gave me six pairs of tiny
caterpillar eyes, and
holes in my side
to breathe.

In my cozy chrysalis
I became a gooey mess—
saved some parts, turned others
to ooze—then I built a brand
new body, and a pair of
splendid wings.

Now I'm a monarch
butterfly, and I know it's
quite bizarre, but I really do use
my antennae to smell, and
my legs and feet
to taste.

And would you believe,
the aerodynamic magic of
my bold and beautiful wings
is thanks to thousands of
tiny, colorful…scales?
(I am not a snake.)

You might think I'm
nature's mixed-up miracle,
but that's okay…I know
I'm built the way
I'm meant
to be.

Joan Duris

THE JOURNEY

Clouds of orange descend
Shimmering treetop blankets:
Monarch migration

CYNTHIA GREENE

ABOUT THE CONTRIBUTOR

As a child, Cindy Greene wanted to be Shel Silverstein, a kindergarten art teacher, or the president of the World Bank. While not on track for any of those, she loves to write poetry and picture books and make things. Cindy helps non-profits with strategy and metrics, works on issues of racial justice, and spends loads of time with her fun family. She spends much of the day laughing.

Cindy's poetry can be found in several anthologies and stamped in a concrete sidewalk in her town.

UNTITLED

like fall leaves, monarchs
face the gravity
of their migration

ROYAL TREATMENT

In the restaurant window,
the monarch flutters frantically.
She is capable of migrating thousands of miles,
but now glass blocks her from flying
ten feet to the garden.
Fretful over her captivity, she desperately beats her delicate wings.

A glint of her regal marigold
catches a passing child's eye.
Understanding her struggle,
her spirit,
he wriggles from his mother's hand
and runs to open the door.
Like a loyal servant, he kneels,
cups his hands, and
gently guides her outside to freedom.

The monarch's flight is a curtsy of thanks.
The boy nods as she glides into the flowers.

JON HARRIS

ABOUT THE CONTRIBUTOR

Jon Harris was born in Coos Bay, Oregon, and grew up on the Oregon Coast. He started writing poetry in high school and later graduated from North Bend High School. Now, he resides in Portland, Oregon, with his wife Anna, and is currently enrolled at Portland Community College, pursuing studies in creative writing and psychology. Harris has a haiku gallery on Instagram, and his page is called Harris Haiku (@jonharris7717). Hey Hey Books is his first poetry publication.

UNTITLED

We are butterflies.
We can't dwell on mistakes made
as caterpillars.

LYN JEKOWSKY

ABOUT THE CONTRIBUTOR

Writing, from journaling to composing my memoir, has always been a part of who I am. My 36-year practice as a pediatric nurse inspired me to write children's books and poetry, to provide them with tools to journey through life. I participate in a critique group, work with a writing partner, and am an active member of SCBWI, Julie Hedlund's 12x12 Picture Book Challenge, and two other professional writing organizations. As a certified children's yoga instructor, I often base postures and meditations on picture books. When I'm not writing, you can find me at the beach, in my garden, or walking my beloved yellow lab.

PLAYFUL BUTTERFLY

A color surprise.
Wings flutter, tickly my nose,
Round antennae bob.

MONARCH WANDERER

Double-winged color
Lacy black on orange wings
In clusters take flight
Migratory corridor
Seasonal phenomenon

BUTTERFLY BEATS

Winged color pulsates
Antennae like pendulums
Join with my heartbeat

MONARCH

Metamorphosis,
black and orange wings unfurl.
New pollinator.

MICHELLE KOGAN

ABOUT THE CONTRIBUTOR

Michelle Kogan ponders petals, beauty, nature and humanity as a poet, writer, artist, and instructor. Her poems are published in many children's and adult anthologies. She was a semi-finalist for the Poet's Billow 2021 *Bermuda Triangle Prize*. In her writing and art, nature always seems to call her, along with social injustices and inequalities for humans, flora, fauna, and our endangered small planet. Presently she's working on a poetry and art bird book. Find more of Michelle's writing and art here:

Website: www.michellekogan.com

Blog: www.moreart4all.wordpress.com

Instagram handle: @mkogancreate

Twitter: @MichelleKogan

Michelle Kogan

PINING FOR MONARCH

Oh my butterfly
how I pine for your sight,
ponder on by and
pay me a visit soon,
don't make me wait till June…

FOREVER'S AN AWFUL LONG TIME

They tell us we have 10–12 years
and then global climate change
will have beyond-devastating effects

But it's already happening now,
February feels like it's been forever…
Ice, snow, polar vortex cold, and it crawls on–

I keep on painting milkweed from my garden
I had an incredible crop last summer, but overall,
they're on the decline, down some 90%

But I keep on painting them because
I want more monarchs to populate, and perhaps
exhibiting my paintings will get more folks involved…

When the milkweed flowers, it attracts
all different kinds of bees, moths, other butterflies,
milkweed beetles, and other insects

If you saw a large group of monarchs feeding on
the milkweed, fluttering, floating up on wisps of air,
and then drifting down again–it's breathless

We could learn something from these
milkweed plants, and help the planet
all at the same time–Somehow, we need to

convince the farmers and other folks
along the monarchs' path to grow milkweed,
So we don't lose these pollinators forever

forever's an awful long time…

ACT NOW

Monarch
butterflies are
a fabulous part of the
invertebrate animal family.

Like gossamer warriors they
migrate thousands of miles between
homes.

Monarchs are important pollinators. While
feeding on nectar they unknowingly move pollen
around flowers. This helps flowers make seeds, and
these seeds travel and eventually grow into new plants.

They bring beauty to our gardens and solace to our hectic
lives with their fascinating flutters and lovely lilting swooops.

Let's steer monarchs off the endangered list by planting native
milkweed and other native pollinating plants. Let's keep pesticides,
herbicides, and inorganic fertilizers out of gardens and farm fields
to help protect monarchs, and reclaim their lost habitat. Let's do this
together so many more generations   of monarchs will flourish, and
many more generations of   children will experience
monarch's moving sense   of wonder, and deep value
to us all!

PAPILIO POLYXENES–HYBRID PERCEPTION

"The genus name 'Papilio' is the Latin word for butterfly."

You're Beautiful

Polyxenes comes "from Polyxena, the daughter of Priamos,
King of Troy (Homer's Iliad)."

Some say you are a pest–eating farmers' and gardeners' fields…
Your pest part belongs to your lineage before your metamorphosis.
When you were a caterpillar, you nibbled away on carrot tops and
its family of dill, parsley, fennel, and Queen Anne's lace.
But you, dear swallow tail, are no pest,
you are magnificent…
And you bring pollination treasures,
beauty, and moments of reflection.

You offer a gift of flutter and escape,
Alighting lightly on my milkweed and zinnias…
And I will always wonder of your wounded antenna–
How it came to be in your short, short life–approximately 12 days
I discovered you in perfect form except for your antenna.

I'm curious to know why you were named after Polyxena,
the Greek princess who bravely accepted her sacrifice
at age 18 for the lost life of Achilles.
Perhaps your shared beauty connects
you through time…

Carry us away, beautiful black swallowtail butterfly…

JULI MAYER

ABOUT THE CONTRIBUTOR

Juli Mayer is a children's poet. She has been published in Highlights, Highlights High Five, The School Magazine (Australia), Boys Quest and also has poems in the poetry anthology *Hop To It: Poems To Get You Moving* and *Things We Feel* edited by Janet Wong and Sylvia Vardell. She was a teacher for hearing-impaired children and a college educational sign language interpreter. Last summer, Juli, her daughter, and her toddler grandchild shared in the wonder of watching a monarch butterfly emerge from its chrysalis. You can follow her on Twitter @JuliMayer2644

MONARCH MARKINGS

Here's the difference between males and females—
Just check out these subtle details.
On each hind wing of the male—there is a black spot,
but the almost identical female does not.
Males can be slightly larger, as well.
That's also a way you can tell.
Females have thicker veining, too.
This can be another clue.
Now, you know how to tell them apart.
They're not just a wonderful work of art.
Monarchs have identifying features
to designate each beloved creature.

MONARCH BUTTERFLY'S BEAUTY

The magnificent Monarch's
vivid orange wings with black veins
reminds me of a church's
stained glass window panes.

HOW TO HELP THE
MONARCH BUTTERFLY

Be proactive, be the spark.
Let's help the magnificent Monarch!

In a sunny spot, plant native milkweeds
where Monarchs lay their eggs and caterpillars feed.
Then the caterpillars transform into chrysalis.
After about two weeks, Monarchs emerge from this.

Be proactive, be the spark.
Let's help the magnificent Monarch.
Don't let their future be a question mark!

GARRETT PAUL

ABOUT THE CONTRIBUTOR

Garrett Paul grew up in Texas and moved to Alabama, where he finished high school. Along with science courses, creative writing classes were his favorite. He went on to start his undergraduate neuroscience degree at UAB. He enjoys writing in his free time and plans to do more as he finishes college.

MY WINGS SPREAD LIKE
THE MORNING DEW

My wings spread like the morning dew

They bathe in the sun, so warm and so bright

Stretch, stretch, stretch

My wings, a gift of color

For the sky, which sits so bare and grey

They wave to the sun

Flutter, flutter

My wings lift me through the air

Met by a thousand gentle hugs from the air around them

Fly

A final wave goodbye to the ground, can never wave back

PAMELA B. TAYLOR

ABOUT THE CONTRIBUTOR

Farm life taught Pamela B. Taylor to care for the earth before becoming a teacher and reading specialist. She shared her passion for nature with young students in the classroom. Collecting and feeding monarch caterpillars was a favorite unit of study! Now, she creates pun-filled tales, poetry, and quirky animal adventures. She is especially excited about her poems "Migration" and "Metamorphosis" being included in *Fly*. Pamela has other poems featured in multiple anthologies by Vardell and Wong and included in a future issue of *LADYBUG Magazine*. When she is not writing, she enjoys hiking, reading, and crafts. https://pamelabtaylor.com

Pamela B. Taylor

METAMORPHOSIS

We grow, we change.
Our cells rearrange.
We welcome each stage.
It's how we all age!

MIRIAM WADE

ABOUT THE CONTRIBUTOR

Miriam Wade is a Minnesota local who writes young adult fantasy, adventure, and urban fantasy driven by resilient young women, filled with twisty plots, and garnished with a hint of romance. She loves coffee, playing video games, and riding her bicycle. When she is not writing, she enjoys spending time with her husband, their two young daughters, and their cat. Wade is the author of the award-winning steampunk Arthurian inspired series, *One Sword Saga*, and the forthcoming paranormal urban fantasy, *The Woman of Blythe Manor*, as well as a featured poet in several anthologies.

Instagram: www.instagram.com/miriam.wade.author

Facebook: www.facebook.com/miriam.wade.author

Twitter: www.twitter.com/wade_author

TikTok: www.tiktok.com/@miriam.wade.author

Website: www.miriam-wade.com

BUTTERFLY

Butterflies flit and flutter with grace,
Unfolding wings of delicate lace.
The air alive with their vibrant hue,
Taking flight as they bid adieu.
Ephemeral beauty, a royal dynasty.
Radiant colors, a joyful melody,
Fluttering free, a whimsical symphony.
Lacy wings, a wonder to behold,
Yet delicate, they are truly gold.

LIKE ROYALTY

Amidst the fields and gardens, they appear,
The monarch butterflies with wings so grand,
Their orange and black hues so bright and clear,
Like royalty, they rule the sky and land.

Upon the wings of orange, black, and white,
The monarch butterfly takes to the air,
A royal creature, such a wondrous sight,
As if a king or queen, beyond compare.

Its journey long, across the open land,
Guided by instincts, a true monarch's grace,
A noble quest, as if a regal command,
Its fragile wings, such elegance and pace.

So, like a monarch, it commands respect,
A royal butterfly perfect in every aspect.

MOONLIGHT

Moths flutter by the moonlight's glow,
Out of the darkness, they seem to grow,
On silent wings, they come and go.
Night's creatures that we embrace,
Lighting up the darkness, they grace,
Intricate patterns on wings they trace.
Glimmering stars in the dark of night,
Hovering like ghosts, they take to flight,
The flutter of wings, in the pale moonlight.

Margarette Wahl

ABOUT THE CONTRIBUTOR

Margarette Wahl has been a Special Education Teacher Aide for over twenty years on Long Island.

She's a member of the Bards Initiative and an Advisor for the Nassau County Poet Laureate Society.

She has four chapbooks of poetry with Local Gems Press and published in a number of Anthologies. She adores Monarch butterflies which compelled her to submit to this Anthology.

BUTTERFLY WISHES

Three butterflies,
three wishes I made for you
Colorful moths,
flowers that can fly
on gossamer wings.
Love's winged messengers.

Painted ladies flutter
while they listen
with their wings,
taste with their legs,
smell with antennae.
I sense you while we are apart.

Pollen is a source of seduction.
Flowers open for butterflies.
Like flowers, I wait
to see you once more.
Flame azaleas give swallowtails
their color.

Queen and Monarch butterflies
use milkweed to warn off predators.
Butterflies live in constant danger.
Hope you are safe like these winged insects
until our next encounter.

Even at Summer's end
I feel you near
on the wind's breath
soaring with the blowing of
butterflies' migration.

MIKE WAHL

ABOUT THE CONTRIBUTOR

Mike retired in 2013 after a 48-year career as an Aerospace Engineer, but continues to work on his organic farm. Writing is a more recent passion than farming, but those efforts often include agrarian aspects. With writing efforts concentrated primarily on poetry, Mike is a member of several poetry organizations in Alabama. Mike's poems have appeared in numerous print and online venues in recent years, plus the annual Best Poets anthologies in the last five years. Poem subjects consist of aspects from farming, nature, social issues, politics, religion, and family interactions. Mike has three books of published poetry: *Living Adverbially* (March 2020), *Rooted in Christianity* (September 2021), and *In Harmony with Homophones* (December 2021).

Mike Wahl

FLIGHT PATH

the air feels Fallish, for real this time,
but that is only apropos,
with days having slipped past
the Autumnal Equinox a month ago;

monarchs as messengers float along on the chill,
as if unable to flap too-stiff wings,
but when the breeze gives its energy,
that saves the kings;

they are singles, all bound for the same destination,
not like blackbirds, bunched into noisy flocks,
instead, migrating steadily ahead,
guided by internal compasses and clocks;

from the hill-side, where the still-green leaves
half hide the view of the valley's peace,
minds may still stretch into what the eyes perceive:
the orange and black pattern that seemingly won't cease;

hundreds, nay thousands, all along this route,
on a journey to a promised land they've never seen,
where colonies of millions tinge fir mountain forests
in central Mexico with an orangish sheen;

there's a flight plan that has never been filed,
a flight path that's never been rehearsed,
and a specific place for months of winter rest,
until Springtime, when it all will be reversed.

MILKWEED

borne by the breeze,
white wisps of fluff float past,
too numerous to track,
each clutching beneath it
a small brown seed that will become
tomorrow's milkweed plant;

today's milkweed plant is broadcasting
its DNA alert,
selected from spiny pods along the stem
that have split open easily
by mere maturity,
revealing white wisps of fluff
attached to small brown seeds
that are its unique heritage;

neatly, compactly folded next to neighbors,
fluff and seed conjoined for their mission:
go far and grow well,
inundating acres at a time,
for next year's banquet spread:

the only thing they'll eat,
a feast for monarch caterpillars.

SASSIE

Sassie.
It's the name of the cow he milks daily.
Her calf was born two weeks ago,
on the fourth of July, a heifer,
light brown, like Sassie.
Apparently, her shape, or the color
attracted unusual visitors:

when he first found the calf,
asleep in the tall grass,
Sassie stood close by, in the full sun,
as was a mother's prerogative,
chewing her cud and ignoring
the three monarchs,
like ornaments,
perched along the calf's back.

CONTEST WINNERS

THE BUTTERFLY NET
by Joan Duris

Families

      tiptoe through

         fluttering fields

  S

    W

      I

       S

CAPTURE!

        H

  Spot

         H

  closeup

         H

  clues…then   release.

Slow dance continues, tiptoe

tasting in graceful

     flower-to-flower

zig-zags.

MIGRATION
by Pamela B. Taylor

Mexico, the mecca of
Overwintering
Navigators of orange and black
Aerial acrobats who
Return to
Colonies at their ancestral
Habitat

EAT YOUR GREENS
by Pamela B. Taylor

It's time for you to eat your greens.
Use instinct now. It's in your genes.
You're a new caterpillar who needs protein.
Eat milkweed leaves — the best cuisine!

We know you are a young beginner,
but don't expect a catered dinner!
You must grow or you'll get thinner.
Now show us you can be a winner!

You need good food to be a butterfly.
Do not skimp now — you have to try!
And watch for enemies from the sky,
so hide in the weed that you occupy!

You'll rest and change by natural means.
That's why you should just…
      "Eat your greens!"

80

UNTITLED

by Miriam Wade

Majestic in its towering stance,
Its blooms a haven for butterflies, a chance
Luring them in with its fragrant call,
Kindred spirits, a dance with them all.
Weaving a tapestry of green and gold,
Ephemeral beauty, but a sight to behold.
Exquisite in form, a natural art,
Dwelling in a garden, a vibrant part.

COMING
SOON

The following is an excerpt.
Wild will be available as an eBook and a paperback.

Wild

Untitled

out of tree crumbs
tiny mushrooms stake
their umbrellas

— Marcie Flinchum Atkins

so much green

nature is resilient
and wise,
she does not need us
yet she has always
been kind to me;

perhaps she recognizes
the wilds in me that they
are always trying to tame or
tell me to swallow down—

i hear the music in the wings
of honey and bumble bees,
feel the compassion of trees,
appreciate the wings of birds in
flight;

once a majestic crow
welcomed me into the forest
and you cannot convince me
there is no magic in a place
where there is so much life and
so much green.

— Linda M. Crate

CAROLINA WREN (WC: 36)

"Tea-kettle, tea-kettle, tea!"
Calls the Carolina Wren.

Reminds me of a rooster's crow,
Again, again, and again.

Wren perches on a high tree branch,
And throws back his little head,

"Tea-kettle, tea-kettle, tea!"
Calls the Carolina Wren.

— Leslie Degnan

IF TREES COULD TALK

If trees
could talk, would they
whisper like wind on moss,
or rumble greetings, deep and slow?
HELLO-O-O-O.

If trees
could dance, would they
twirl lightly through the woods,
or thump around on gnarly feet?
SWEET.   BEAT.

If trees
could smell, would they
gently sniff hints of spring,
or inhale worlds of sneezy scents?
ACHOO-O-O-O!

— Joan Duris

Happiness

Someone always leaves
muddy boots by the door,
he says.

And it's always me,
I realize, a smile
on my face.

— Loria Harris

The Goldfinch

The goldfinch never
wonders of the impact
of what she creates.

She is also unaware
she creates a scene
of absolute wonder.

— Andy Perrin

Untitled

Sunlight warms us as
leaves cast eyelet-lace shadows
on the hiking path.

— Susan Johnson Taylor

Acknowledgements

To Marcie Flinchum Atkins, Benjamin Bishop, Patricia Cooley, Linda M. Crate, Robert Daniel. Leslie Degnan, Linda A. Dryfhout, Joan Duris, Cynthia Greene, Jon Harris, Lyn Jekoswky, Michelle Kogan, Juli Mayer, Garrett Paul, Pamela B. Taylor, Miriam Wade, Margarette Wahl, and Mike Wahl, thank you for showcasing your exceptional work. *Fly* would not be here today without your generous contribution.

The publication of *Fly* would not have been possible without a few more contributors. A special thank you to Jeanette Barroso (cover designer), Elise Pullen (illustrator), and Alyssa Myers (editor).

Thank you, reader, for taking the time to divulge in these poems.

If you are interested in further support for monarchs, please consider visiting these sites:

www.saveourmonarchs.org
www.monarchjointventure.org

Most importantly, we give thanks to the butterflies for inspiring this anthology. Without them, our yards would be desolate.

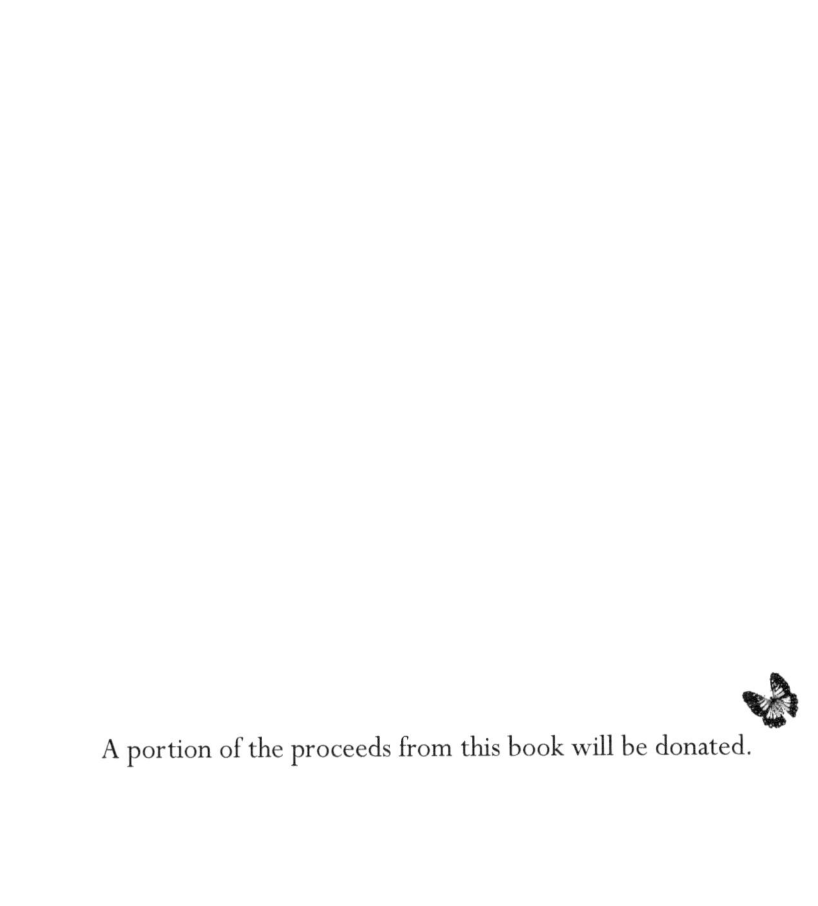

A portion of the proceeds from this book will be donated.

9 798218 227623